SMALL BUSINESS C
LOG BOOK

Your Name : _____

Phone No : _____

Email : _____

Social Media : _____

Website : _____

Address : _____

Business Name : _____

Date Founded : _____

Department : _____

Start Date : _____

— IF THE —

Plan

DOESN'T

WORK

· CHANGE THE PLAN ·

BUT NEVER THE

GOAL

Table Of Content

2022

January

S	M	T	W	T	F	S
						1
2	3	4	5	6	7	8
9	10	11	12	13	14	15
16	17	18	19	20	21	22
23	24	25	26	27	28	29
30	31					

February

S	M	T	W	T	F	S
		1	2	3	4	5
6	7	8	9	10	11	12
13	14	15	16	17	18	19
20	21	22	23	24	25	26
27	28					

March

S	M	T	W	T	F	S
		1	2	3	4	5
6	7	8	9	10	11	12
13	14	15	16	17	18	19
20	21	22	23	24	25	26
27	28	29	30	31		

April

S	M	T	W	T	F	S
					1	2
3	4	5	6	7	8	9
10	11	12	13	14	15	16
17	18	19	20	21	22	23
24	25	26	27	28	29	30

May

S	M	T	W	T	F	S
1	2	3	4	5	6	7
8	9	10	11	12	13	14
15	16	17	18	19	20	21
22	23	24	25	26	27	28
29	30	31				

June

S	M	T	W	T	F	S
			1	2	3	4
5	6	7	8	9	10	11
12	13	14	15	16	17	18
19	20	21	22	23	24	25
26	27	28	29	30		

July

S	M	T	W	T	F	S
					1	2
3	4	5	6	7	8	9
10	11	12	13	14	15	16
17	18	19	20	21	22	23
24	25	26	27	28	29	30
31						

August

S	M	T	W	T	F	S
	1	2	3	4	5	6
7	8	9	10	11	12	13
14	15	16	17	18	19	20
21	22	23	24	25	26	27
28	29	30	31			

September

S	M	T	W	T	F	S
				1	2	3
4	5	6	7	8	9	10
11	12	13	14	15	16	17
18	19	20	21	22	23	24
25	26	27	28	29	30	

October

S	M	T	W	T	F	S
						1
2	3	4	5	6	7	8
9	10	11	12	13	14	15
16	17	18	19	20	21	22
23	24	25	26	27	28	29
30	31					

November

S	M	T	W	T	F	S
		1	2	3	4	5
6	7	8	9	10	11	12
13	14	15	16	17	18	19
20	21	22	23	24	25	26
27	28	29	30			

December

S	M	T	W	T	F	S
				1	2	3
4	5	6	7	8	9	10
11	12	13	14	15	16	17
18	19	20	21	22	23	24
25	26	27	28	29	30	31

ANNUAL OVERVIEW

Year-

January	February	March
April	May	June
July	August	September
October	November	December

BUSINESS GOAL

Goal	Steps To Take	Achieved

Deadline -

BUSINESS GOAL

Goal	Steps To Take	Achieved

Deadline -

SUPPLIERS CONTACTS

Name _____

Business _____

Website _____

Email _____

Phone _____

Name _____

Business _____

Website _____

Email _____

Phone _____

Name _____

Business _____

Website _____

Email _____

Phone _____

Name _____

Business _____

Website _____

Email _____

Phone _____

Name _____

Business _____

Website _____

Email _____

Phone _____

Name _____

Business _____

Website _____

Email _____

Phone _____

Name _____

Business _____

Website _____

Email _____

Phone _____

Name _____

Business _____

Website _____

Email _____

Phone _____

SUPPLIERS CONTACTS

Name _____

Business _____

Website _____

Email _____

Phone _____

Name _____

Business _____

Website _____

Email _____

Phone _____

Name _____

Business _____

Website _____

Email _____

Phone _____

Name _____

Business _____

Website _____

Email _____

Phone _____

Name _____

Business _____

Website _____

Email _____

Phone _____

Name _____

Business _____

Website _____

Email _____

Phone _____

Name _____

Business _____

Website _____

Email _____

Phone _____

Name _____

Business _____

Website _____

Email _____

Phone _____

SUPPLIERS CONTACTS

Name _____

Business _____

Website _____

Email _____

Phone _____

Name _____

Business _____

Website _____

Email _____

Phone _____

Name _____

Business _____

Website _____

Email _____

Phone _____

Name _____

Business _____

Website _____

Email _____

Phone _____

Name _____

Business _____

Website _____

Email _____

Phone _____

Name _____

Business _____

Website _____

Email _____

Phone _____

Name _____

Business _____

Website _____

Email _____

Phone _____

Name _____

Business _____

Website _____

Email _____

Phone _____

SUPPLY LIST

Item Needed	Supplier	Cost	Qty	Total	Ordered	Received

SUPPLY LIST

Item Needed	Supplier	Cost	Qty	Total	Ordered	Received

SUPPLY LIST

Item Needed	Supplier	Cost	Qty	Total	Ordered	Received

PRODUCT INVENTORY

Date	Product	Qty	Cost	Sell	Profit

Note :

PRODUCT INVENTORY

Date	Product	Qty	Cost	Sell	Profit

Note :

PRODUCT INVENTORY

Date	Product	Qty	Cost	Sell	Profit

Note :

PRODUCT INVENTORY

Date	Product	Qty	Cost	Sell	Profit

Note :

PRODUCT INVENTORY

Date	Product	Qty	Cost	Sell	Profit

Note :

PRODUCT INVENTORY

Date	Product	Qty	Cost	Sell	Profit

Note :

PRODUCT INVENTORY

Date	Product	Qty	Cost	Sell	Profit

Note :

PRODUCT INVENTORY

Date	Product	Qty	Cost	Sell	Profit

Note :

PRODUCT INVENTORY

Date	Product	Qty	Cost	Sell	Profit

Note :

PRODUCT INVENTORY

Date	Product	Qty	Cost	Sell	Profit

Note :

COST & PROFIT RECORD

Product	Cost	Fees	Shipping	Sale Price	Profit

COST & PROFIT RECORD

Product	Cost	Fees	Shipping	Sale Price	Profit

COST & PROFIT RECORD

Product	Cost	Fees	Shipping	Sale Price	Profit

COST & PROFIT RECORD

Product	Cost	Fees	Shipping	Sale Price	Profit

COST & PROFIT RECORD

Product	Cost	Fees	Shipping	Sale Price	Profit

COST & PROFIT RECORD

Product	Cost	Fees	Shipping	Sale Price	Profit

COST & PROFIT RECORD

Product	Cost	Fees	Shipping	Sale Price	Profit

COST & PROFIT RECORD

Product	Cost	Fees	Shipping	Sale Price	Profit

COST & PROFIT RECORD

Product	Cost	Fees	Shipping	Sale Price	Profit

COST & PROFIT RECORD

Product	Cost	Fees	Shipping	Sale Price	Profit

ORDER TRACKER

Date	Order	Customer	Qty	Item	Shipping Day

ORDER TRACKER

Date	Order	Customer	Qty	Item	Shipping Day

ORDER TRACKER

Date	Order	Customer	Qty	Item	Shipping Day

DATE :

ORDER NO :

 ORDER FORM

CUSTOMER NAME _____

ADDRESS _____

EMAIL _____ PHONE _____

ITEM NO	ITEM DESCRIPTION	QTY.	UNIT PRICE	TOTAL PRICE

SHPPING METHOD _____

SHIPPING COMPANY _____

TRACKING IN _____

SHIPPING DATE _____

ARRIVAL DATE _____

SUBTOTAL _____

DISCOUNT _____

TAXES _____

SHIPPING _____

TOTAL _____

NOTE :

DATE :

ORDER NO :

 ORDER FORM

CUSTOMER NAME _____

ADDRESS _____

EMAIL _____ PHONE _____

ITEM NO	ITEM DESCRIPTION	QTY.	UNIT PRICE	TOTAL PRICE

SHPPING METHOD _____

SHIPPING COMPANY _____

TRACKING IN _____

SHIPPING DATE _____

ARRIVAL DATE _____

SUBTOTAL _____

DISCOUNT _____

TAXES _____

SHIPPING _____

TOTAL _____

NOTE :

DATE :

ORDER NO :

 ORDER FORM

CUSTOMER NAME _____

ADDRESS _____

EMAIL _____ PHONE _____

ITEM NO	ITEM DESCRIPTION	QTY.	UNIT PRICE	TOTAL PRICE

SHPPING METHOD _____

SHIPPING COMPANY _____

TRACKING IN _____

SHIPPING DATE _____

ARRIVAL DATE _____

SUBTOTAL _____

DISCOUNT _____

TAXES _____

SHIPPING _____

TOTAL _____

NOTE :

DATE :

ORDER NO :

ORDER FORM

CUSTOMER NAME _____

ADDRESS _____

EMAIL _____ PHONE _____

ITEM NO	ITEM DESCRIPTION	QTY.	UNIT PRICE	TOTAL PRICE

SHPPING METHOD _____

SHIPPING COMPANY _____

TRACKING IN _____

SHIPPING DATE _____

ARRIVAL DATE _____

SUBTOTAL _____

DISCOUNT _____

TAXES _____

SHIPPING _____

TOTAL _____

NOTE :

DATE :

ORDER NO :

 ORDER FORM

CUSTOMER NAME _____

ADDRESS _____

EMAIL _____ PHONE _____

ITEM NO	ITEM DESCRIPTION	QTY.	UNIT PRICE	TOTAL PRICE

SHPPING METHOD _____

SHIPPING COMPANY _____

TRACKING IN _____

SHIPPING DATE _____

ARRIVAL DATE _____

SUBTOTAL _____

DISCOUNT _____

TAXES _____

SHIPPING _____

TOTAL _____

NOTE :

DATE :

ORDER NO :

ORDER FORM

CUSTOMER NAME _____

ADDRESS _____

EMAIL _____ PHONE _____

ITEM NO	ITEM DESCRIPTION	QTY.	UNIT PRICE	TOTAL PRICE

SHPPING METHOD _____

SHIPPING COMPANY _____

TRACKING IN _____

SHIPPING DATE _____

ARRIVAL DATE _____

SUBTOTAL _____

DISCOUNT _____

TAXES _____

SHIPPING _____

TOTAL _____

NOTE :

DATE :

ORDER NO :

ORDER FORM

CUSTOMER NAME _____

ADDRESS _____

EMAIL _____ PHONE _____

ITEM NO	ITEM DESCRIPTION	QTY.	UNIT PRICE	TOTAL PRICE

SHPPING METHOD _____

SHIPPING COMPANY _____

TRACKING IN _____

SHIPPING DATE _____

ARRIVAL DATE _____

SUBTOTAL _____

DISCOUNT _____

TAXES _____

SHIPPING _____

TOTAL _____

NOTE :

DATE :

ORDER NO :

 ORDER FORM

CUSTOMER NAME _____

ADDRESS _____

EMAIL _____ PHONE _____

ITEM NO	ITEM DESCRIPTION	QTY.	UNIT PRICE	TOTAL PRICE

SHPPING METHOD _____

SHIPPING COMPANY _____

TRACKING IN _____

SHIPPING DATE _____

ARRIVAL DATE _____

SUBTOTAL _____

DISCOUNT _____

TAXES _____

SHIPPING _____

TOTAL _____

NOTE :

DATE :

ORDER NO :

ORDER FORM

CUSTOMER NAME _____

ADDRESS _____

EMAIL _____ PHONE _____

ITEM NO	ITEM DESCRIPTION	QTY.	UNIT PRICE	TOTAL PRICE

SHPPING METHOD _____

SHIPPING COMPANY _____

TRACKING IN _____

SHIPPING DATE _____

ARRIVAL DATE _____

SUBTOTAL _____

DISCOUNT _____

TAXES _____

SHIPPING _____

TOTAL _____

NOTE :

DATE :
ORDER NO :

ORDER FORM

CUSTOMER NAME _____

ADDRESS _____

EMAIL _____ PHONE _____

ITEM NO	ITEM DESCRIPTION	QTY.	UNIT PRICE	TOTAL PRICE

SHPPING METHOD _____

SHIPPING COMPANY _____

TRACKING IN _____

SHIPPING DATE _____

ARRIVAL DATE _____

SUBTOTAL _____

DISCOUNT _____

TAXES _____

SHIPPING _____

TOTAL _____

NOTE :

DATE :

ORDER NO:

 ORDER FORM

CUSTOMER NAME _____

ADDRESS _____

EMAIL _____ PHONE _____

ITEM NO	ITEM DESCRIPTION	QTY.	UNIT PRICE	TOTAL PRICE

SHPPING METHOD _____

SHIPPING COMPANY _____

TRACKING IN _____

SHIPPING DATE _____

ARRIVAL DATE _____

SUBTOTAL _____

DISCOUNT _____

TAXES _____

SHIPPING _____

TOTAL _____

NOTE :

DATE :

ORDER NO :

 ORDER FORM

CUSTOMER NAME _____

ADDRESS _____

EMAIL _____ PHONE _____

ITEM NO	ITEM DESCRIPTION	QTY.	UNIT PRICE	TOTAL PRICE

SHPPING METHOD _____

SHIPPING COMPANY _____

TRACKING IN _____

SHIPPING DATE _____

ARRIVAL DATE _____

SUBTOTAL _____

DISCOUNT _____

TAXES _____

SHIPPING _____

TOTAL _____

NOTE :

DATE :

ORDER NO :

 ORDER FORM

CUSTOMER NAME _____

ADDRESS _____

EMAIL _____ PHONE _____

ITEM NO	ITEM DESCRIPTION	QTY.	UNIT PRICE	TOTAL PRICE

SHPPING METHOD _____

SHIPPING COMPANY _____

TRACKING IN _____

SHIPPING DATE _____

ARRIVAL DATE _____

SUBTOTAL _____

DISCOUNT _____

TAXES _____

SHIPPING _____

TOTAL _____

NOTE :

DATE :

ORDER NO :

 ORDER FORM

CUSTOMER NAME _____

ADDRESS _____

EMAIL _____ PHONE _____

ITEM NO	ITEM DESCRIPTION	QTY.	UNIT PRICE	TOTAL PRICE

SHPPING METHOD _____

SHIPPING COMPANY _____

TRACKING IN _____

SHIPPING DATE _____

ARRIVAL DATE _____

SUBTOTAL _____

DISCOUNT _____

TAXES _____

SHIPPING _____

TOTAL _____

NOTE :

DATE :

ORDER NO :

 ORDER FORM

CUSTOMER NAME _____

ADDRESS _____

EMAIL _____ PHONE _____

ITEM NO	ITEM DESCRIPTION	QTY.	UNIT PRICE	TOTAL PRICE

SHPPING METHOD _____

SHIPPING COMPANY _____

TRACKING IN _____

SHIPPING DATE _____

ARRIVAL DATE _____

SUBTOTAL _____

DISCOUNT _____

TAXES _____

SHIPPING _____

TOTAL _____

NOTE :

DATE :		 ORDER FORM
ORDER NO :		

CUSTOMER NAME _____

ADDRESS _____

EMAIL _____ **PHONE** _____

ITEM NO	ITEM DESCRIPTION	QTY.	UNIT PRICE	TOTAL PRICE

SHPPING METHOD _____

SHIPPING COMPANY _____

TRACKING IN _____

SHIPPING DATE _____

ARRIVAL DATE _____

SUBTOTAL _____

DISCOUNT _____

TAXES _____

SHIPPING _____

TOTAL _____

NOTE :

DATE :

ORDER NO :

ORDER FORM

CUSTOMER NAME _____

ADDRESS _____

EMAIL _____ PHONE _____

ITEM NO	ITEM DESCRIPTION	QTY.	UNIT PRICE	TOTAL PRICE

SHPPING METHOD _____

SHIPPING COMPANY _____

TRACKING IN _____

SHIPPING DATE _____

ARRIVAL DATE _____

SUBTOTAL _____

DISCOUNT _____

TAXES _____

SHIPPING _____

TOTAL _____

NOTE :

| DATE : |
| ORDER NO : |

ORDER FORM

CUSTOMER NAME _____

ADDRESS _____

EMAIL _____ PHONE _____

ITEM NO	ITEM DESCRIPTION	QTY.	UNIT PRICE	TOTAL PRICE

SHPPING METHOD _____

SHIPPING COMPANY _____

TRACKING IN _____

SHIPPING DATE _____

ARRIVAL DATE _____

SUBTOTAL _____

DISCOUNT _____

TAXES _____

SHIPPING _____

TOTAL _____

NOTE :

DATE :

ORDER NO :

 ORDER FORM

CUSTOMER NAME _____

ADDRESS _____

EMAIL _____ PHONE _____

ITEM NO	ITEM DESCRIPTION	QTY.	UNIT PRICE	TOTAL PRICE

SHPPING METHOD _____

SHIPPING COMPANY _____

TRACKING IN _____

SHIPPING DATE _____

ARRIVAL DATE _____

SUBTOTAL _____

DISCOUNT _____

TAXES _____

SHIPPING _____

TOTAL _____

NOTE :

| DATE : |
| ORDER NO : |

ORDER FORM

CUSTOMER NAME _____

ADDRESS _____

EMAIL _____ PHONE _____

ITEM NO	ITEM DESCRIPTION	QTY.	UNIT PRICE	TOTAL PRICE

SHPPING METHOD _____

SHIPPING COMPANY _____

TRACKING IN _____

SHIPPING DATE _____

ARRIVAL DATE _____

SUBTOTAL _____

DISCOUNT _____

TAXES _____

SHIPPING _____

TOTAL _____

NOTE :

DATE :

ORDER NO :

 ORDER FORM

CUSTOMER NAME _____

ADDRESS _____

EMAIL _____ PHONE _____

ITEM NO	ITEM DESCRIPTION	QTY.	UNIT PRICE	TOTAL PRICE

SHPPING METHOD _____

SHIPPING COMPANY _____

TRACKING IN _____

SHIPPING DATE _____

ARRIVAL DATE _____

SUBTOTAL _____

DISCOUNT _____

TAXES _____

SHIPPING _____

TOTAL _____

NOTE :

DATE :

ORDER NO :

 ORDER FORM

CUSTOMER NAME _____

ADDRESS _____

EMAIL _____ PHONE _____

ITEM NO	ITEM DESCRIPTION	QTY.	UNIT PRICE	TOTAL PRICE

SHPPING METHOD _____

SHIPPING COMPANY _____

TRACKING IN _____

SHIPPING DATE _____

ARRIVAL DATE _____

SUBTOTAL _____

DISCOUNT _____

TAXES _____

SHIPPING _____

TOTAL _____

NOTE :

DATE :

ORDER NO :

ORDER FORM

CUSTOMER NAME _____

ADDRESS _____

EMAIL _____ PHONE _____

ITEM NO	ITEM DESCRIPTION	QTY.	UNIT PRICE	TOTAL PRICE

SHPPING METHOD _____

SHIPPING COMPANY _____

TRACKING IN _____

SHIPPING DATE _____

ARRIVAL DATE _____

SUBTOTAL _____

DISCOUNT _____

TAXES _____

SHIPPING _____

TOTAL _____

NOTE :

DATE :

ORDER NO :

 ORDER FORM

CUSTOMER NAME _____

ADDRESS _____

EMAIL _____ PHONE _____

ITEM NO	ITEM DESCRIPTION	QTY.	UNIT PRICE	TOTAL PRICE

SHPPING METHOD _____

SHIPPING COMPANY _____

TRACKING IN _____

SHIPPING DATE _____

ARRIVAL DATE _____

SUBTOTAL _____

DISCOUNT _____

TAXES _____

SHIPPING _____

TOTAL _____

NOTE :

DATE :

ORDER NO :

ORDER FORM

CUSTOMER NAME _____

ADDRESS _____

EMAIL _____ PHONE _____

ITEM NO	ITEM DESCRIPTION	QTY.	UNIT PRICE	TOTAL PRICE

SHPPING METHOD _____

SHIPPING COMPANY _____

TRACKING IN _____

SHIPPING DATE _____

ARRIVAL DATE _____

SUBTOTAL _____

DISCOUNT _____

TAXES _____

SHIPPING _____

TOTAL _____

NOTE :

DATE :

ORDER NO :

 ORDER FORM

CUSTOMER NAME _____

ADDRESS _____

EMAIL _____ PHONE _____

ITEM NO	ITEM DESCRIPTION	QTY.	UNIT PRICE	TOTAL PRICE

SHPPING METHOD _____

SHIPPING COMPANY _____

TRACKING IN _____

SHIPPING DATE _____

ARRIVAL DATE _____

SUBTOTAL _____

DISCOUNT _____

TAXES _____

SHIPPING _____

TOTAL _____

NOTE :

DATE :

ORDER NO :

ORDER FORM

CUSTOMER NAME _____

ADDRESS _____

EMAIL _____ PHONE _____

ITEM NO	ITEM DESCRIPTION	QTY.	UNIT PRICE	TOTAL PRICE

SHPPING METHOD _____

SHIPPING COMPANY _____

TRACKING IN _____

SHIPPING DATE _____

ARRIVAL DATE _____

SUBTOTAL _____

DISCOUNT _____

TAXES _____

SHIPPING _____

TOTAL _____

NOTE :

DATE :

ORDER NO :

ORDER FORM

CUSTOMER NAME _____

ADDRESS _____

EMAIL _____ PHONE _____

ITEM NO	ITEM DESCRIPTION	QTY.	UNIT PRICE	TOTAL PRICE

SHPPING METHOD _____

SHIPPING COMPANY _____

TRACKING IN _____

SHIPPING DATE _____

ARRIVAL DATE _____

SUBTOTAL _____

DISCOUNT _____

TAXES _____

SHIPPING _____

TOTAL _____

NOTE :

DATE :

ORDER NO :

 ORDER FORM

CUSTOMER NAME _____

ADDRESS _____

EMAIL _____ PHONE _____

ITEM NO	ITEM DESCRIPTION	QTY.	UNIT PRICE	TOTAL PRICE

SHPPING METHOD _____

SHIPPING COMPANY _____

TRACKING IN _____

SHIPPING DATE _____

ARRIVAL DATE _____

SUBTOTAL _____

DISCOUNT _____

TAXES _____

SHIPPING _____

TOTAL _____

NOTE :

DATE :

ORDER NO :

ORDER FORM

CUSTOMER NAME _____

ADDRESS _____

EMAIL _____ PHONE _____

ITEM NO	ITEM DESCRIPTION	QTY.	UNIT PRICE	TOTAL PRICE

SHPPING METHOD _____

SHIPPING COMPANY _____

TRACKING IN _____

SHIPPING DATE _____

ARRIVAL DATE _____

SUBTOTAL _____

DISCOUNT _____

TAXES _____

SHIPPING _____

TOTAL _____

NOTE :

DATE :

ORDER NO:

 ORDER FORM

CUSTOMER NAME _____

ADDRESS _____

EMAIL _____ PHONE _____

ITEM NO	ITEM DESCRIPTION	QTY.	UNIT PRICE	TOTAL PRICE

SHPPING METHOD _____

SHIPPING COMPANY _____

TRACKING IN _____

SHIPPING DATE _____

ARRIVAL DATE _____

SUBTOTAL _____

DISCOUNT _____

TAXES _____

SHIPPING _____

TOTAL _____

NOTE :

DATE :

ORDER NO :

 ORDER FORM

CUSTOMER NAME _____

ADDRESS _____

EMAIL _____ PHONE _____

ITEM NO	ITEM DESCRIPTION	QTY.	UNIT PRICE	TOTAL PRICE

SHPPING METHOD _____

SHIPPING COMPANY _____

TRACKING IN _____

SHIPPING DATE _____

ARRIVAL DATE _____

SUBTOTAL _____

DISCOUNT _____

TAXES _____

SHIPPING _____

TOTAL _____

NOTE :

DATE :

ORDER NO :

 ORDER FORM

CUSTOMER NAME _____

ADDRESS _____

EMAIL _____ PHONE _____

ITEM NO	ITEM DESCRIPTION	QTY.	UNIT PRICE	TOTAL PRICE

SHPPING METHOD _____

SHIPPING COMPANY _____

TRACKING IN _____

SHIPPING DATE _____

ARRIVAL DATE _____

SUBTOTAL _____

DISCOUNT _____

TAXES _____

SHIPPING _____

TOTAL _____

NOTE :

DATE :

ORDER NO :

 ORDER FORM

CUSTOMER NAME _____

ADDRESS _____

EMAIL _____ PHONE _____

ITEM NO	ITEM DESCRIPTION	QTY.	UNIT PRICE	TOTAL PRICE

SHPPING METHOD _____

SHIPPING COMPANY _____

TRACKING IN _____

SHIPPING DATE _____

ARRIVAL DATE _____

SUBTOTAL _____

DISCOUNT _____

TAXES _____

SHIPPING _____

TOTAL _____

NOTE :

DATE :

ORDER NO :

 ORDER FORM

CUSTOMER NAME _____

ADDRESS _____

EMAIL _____ PHONE _____

ITEM NO	ITEM DESCRIPTION	QTY.	UNIT PRICE	TOTAL PRICE

SHPPING METHOD _____

SHIPPING COMPANY _____

TRACKING IN _____

SHIPPING DATE _____

ARRIVAL DATE _____

SUBTOTAL _____

DISCOUNT _____

TAXES _____

SHIPPING _____

TOTAL _____

NOTE :

DATE :

ORDER NO :

 ORDER FORM

CUSTOMER NAME _____

ADDRESS _____

EMAIL _____ PHONE _____

ITEM NO	ITEM DESCRIPTION	QTY.	UNIT PRICE	TOTAL PRICE

SHPPING METHOD _____

SHIPPING COMPANY _____

TRACKING IN _____

SHIPPING DATE _____

ARRIVAL DATE _____

SUBTOTAL _____

DISCOUNT _____

TAXES _____

SHIPPING _____

TOTAL _____

NOTE :

DATE :

ORDER NO :

 ORDER FORM

CUSTOMER NAME _____

ADDRESS _____

EMAIL _____ PHONE _____

ITEM NO	ITEM DESCRIPTION	QTY.	UNIT PRICE	TOTAL PRICE

SHPPING METHOD _____

SHIPPING COMPANY _____

TRACKING IN _____

SHIPPING DATE _____

ARRIVAL DATE _____

SUBTOTAL _____

DISCOUNT _____

TAXES _____

SHIPPING _____

TOTAL _____

NOTE :

ORDER FORM

DATE :

ORDER NO :

CUSTOMER NAME _____

ADDRESS _____

EMAIL _____ PHONE _____

ITEM NO	ITEM DESCRIPTION	QTY.	UNIT PRICE	TOTAL PRICE

SHPPING METHOD _____

SHIPPING COMPANY _____

TRACKING IN _____

SHIPPING DATE _____

ARRIVAL DATE _____

SUBTOTAL _____

DISCOUNT _____

TAXES _____

SHIPPING _____

TOTAL _____

NOTE :

DATE :
ORDER NO :

ORDER FORM

CUSTOMER NAME _____

ADDRESS _____

EMAIL _____ PHONE _____

ITEM NO	ITEM DESCRIPTION	QTY.	UNIT PRICE	TOTAL PRICE

SHPPING METHOD _____

SHIPPING COMPANY _____

TRACKING IN _____

SHIPPING DATE _____

ARRIVAL DATE _____

SUBTOTAL _____

DISCOUNT _____

TAXES _____

SHIPPING _____

TOTAL _____

NOTE :

DATE :

ORDER NO :

ORDER FORM

CUSTOMER NAME _____

ADDRESS _____

EMAIL _____ PHONE _____

ITEM NO	ITEM DESCRIPTION	QTY.	UNIT PRICE	TOTAL PRICE

SHPPING METHOD _____

SHIPPING COMPANY _____

TRACKING IN _____

SHIPPING DATE _____

ARRIVAL DATE _____

SUBTOTAL _____

DISCOUNT _____

TAXES _____

SHIPPING _____

TOTAL _____

NOTE :

DATE :

ORDER NO :

 ORDER FORM

CUSTOMER NAME

ADDRESS

EMAIL _____ PHONE _____

ITEM NO	ITEM DESCRIPTION	QTY.	UNIT PRICE	TOTAL PRICE

SHPPING METHOD _____

SHIPPING COMPANY _____

TRACKING IN _____

SHIPPING DATE _____

ARRIVAL DATE _____

SUBTOTAL _____

DISCOUNT _____

TAXES _____

SHIPPING _____

TOTAL _____

NOTE :

DATE :

ORDER NO :

 ORDER FORM

CUSTOMER NAME _____

ADDRESS _____

EMAIL _____ PHONE _____

ITEM NO	ITEM DESCRIPTION	QTY.	UNIT PRICE	TOTAL PRICE

SHPPING METHOD _____

SHIPPING COMPANY _____

TRACKING IN _____

SHIPPING DATE _____

ARRIVAL DATE _____

SUBTOTAL _____

DISCOUNT _____

TAXES _____

SHIPPING _____

TOTAL _____

NOTE :

DATE :

ORDER NO :

 ORDER FORM

CUSTOMER NAME _____

ADDRESS _____

EMAIL _____ PHONE _____

ITEM NO	ITEM DESCRIPTION	QTY.	UNIT PRICE	TOTAL PRICE

SHPPING METHOD _____

SHIPPING COMPANY _____

TRACKING IN _____

SHIPPING DATE _____

ARRIVAL DATE _____

SUBTOTAL _____

DISCOUNT _____

TAXES _____

SHIPPING _____

TOTAL _____

NOTE :

DATE :

ORDER NO :

 ORDER FORM

CUSTOMER NAME _____

ADDRESS _____

EMAIL _____ PHONE _____

ITEM NO	ITEM DESCRIPTION	QTY.	UNIT PRICE	TOTAL PRICE

SHPPING METHOD _____

SHIPPING COMPANY _____

TRACKING IN _____

SHIPPING DATE _____

ARRIVAL DATE _____

SUBTOTAL _____

DISCOUNT _____

TAXES _____

SHIPPING _____

TOTAL _____

NOTE :

DATE :

ORDER NO :

 ORDER FORM

CUSTOMER NAME _____

ADDRESS _____

EMAIL _____ PHONE _____

ITEM NO	ITEM DESCRIPTION	QTY.	UNIT PRICE	TOTAL PRICE

SHPPING METHOD _____

SHIPPING COMPANY _____

TRACKING IN _____

SHIPPING DATE _____

ARRIVAL DATE _____

SUBTOTAL _____

DISCOUNT _____

TAXES _____

SHIPPING _____

TOTAL _____

NOTE :

DATE :

ORDER NO :

 ORDER FORM

CUSTOMER NAME _____

ADDRESS _____

EMAIL _____ PHONE _____

ITEM NO	ITEM DESCRIPTION	QTY.	UNIT PRICE	TOTAL PRICE

SHPPING METHOD _____

SHIPPING COMPANY _____

TRACKING IN _____

SHIPPING DATE _____

ARRIVAL DATE _____

SUBTOTAL _____

DISCOUNT _____

TAXES _____

SHIPPING _____

TOTAL _____

NOTE :

DATE :

ORDER NO :

 ORDER FORM

CUSTOMER NAME

ADDRESS

EMAIL _____ PHONE

ITEM NO	ITEM DESCRIPTION	QTY.	UNIT PRICE	TOTAL PRICE

SHPPING METHOD

SHIPPING COMPANY

TRACKING IN

SHIPPING DATE

ARRIVAL DATE

SUBTOTAL

DISCOUNT

TAXES

SHIPPING

TOTAL

NOTE :

DATE :

ORDER NO :

 ORDER FORM

CUSTOMER NAME _____

ADDRESS _____

EMAIL _____ PHONE _____

ITEM NO	ITEM DESCRIPTION	QTY.	UNIT PRICE	TOTAL PRICE

SHPPING METHOD _____

SHIPPING COMPANY _____

TRACKING IN _____

SHIPPING DATE _____

ARRIVAL DATE _____

SUBTOTAL _____

DISCOUNT _____

TAXES _____

SHIPPING _____

TOTAL _____

NOTE :

DATE :

ORDER NO :

 ORDER FORM

CUSTOMER NAME _____

ADDRESS _____

EMAIL _____ PHONE _____

ITEM NO	ITEM DESCRIPTION	QTY.	UNIT PRICE	TOTAL PRICE

SHPPING METHOD _____

SHIPPING COMPANY _____

TRACKING IN _____

SHIPPING DATE _____

ARRIVAL DATE _____

SUBTOTAL _____

DISCOUNT _____

TAXES _____

SHIPPING _____

TOTAL _____

NOTE :

DATE :

ORDER NO :

 ORDER FORM

CUSTOMER NAME _____

ADDRESS _____

EMAIL _____ PHONE _____

ITEM NO	ITEM DESCRIPTION	QTY.	UNIT PRICE	TOTAL PRICE

SHPPING METHOD _____

SHIPPING COMPANY _____

TRACKING IN _____

SHIPPING DATE _____

ARRIVAL DATE _____

SUBTOTAL _____

DISCOUNT _____

TAXES _____

SHIPPING _____

TOTAL _____

NOTE :

DATE :

ORDER NO :

ORDER FORM

CUSTOMER NAME _____

ADDRESS _____

EMAIL _____ PHONE _____

ITEM NO	ITEM DESCRIPTION	QTY.	UNIT PRICE	TOTAL PRICE

SHPPING METHOD _____

SHIPPING COMPANY _____

TRACKING IN _____

SHIPPING DATE _____

ARRIVAL DATE _____

SUBTOTAL _____

DISCOUNT _____

TAXES _____

SHIPPING _____

TOTAL _____

NOTE :

DATE :

ORDER NO :

ORDER FORM

CUSTOMER NAME _____

ADDRESS _____

EMAIL _____ PHONE _____

ITEM NO	ITEM DESCRIPTION	QTY.	UNIT PRICE	TOTAL PRICE

SHPPING METHOD _____

SHIPPING COMPANY _____

TRACKING IN _____

SHIPPING DATE _____

ARRIVAL DATE _____

SUBTOTAL _____

DISCOUNT _____

TAXES _____

SHIPPING _____

TOTAL _____

NOTE :

DATE :

ORDER NO :

ORDER FORM

CUSTOMER NAME _____

ADDRESS _____

EMAIL _____ PHONE _____

ITEM NO	ITEM DESCRIPTION	QTY.	UNIT PRICE	TOTAL PRICE

SHPPING METHOD _____

SHIPPING COMPANY _____

TRACKING IN _____

SHIPPING DATE _____

ARRIVAL DATE _____

SUBTOTAL _____

DISCOUNT _____

TAXES _____

SHIPPING _____

TOTAL _____

NOTE :

DATE : _____

ORDER NO : _____

 ORDER FORM

CUSTOMER NAME _____

ADDRESS _____

EMAIL _____ PHONE _____

ITEM NO	ITEM DESCRIPTION	QTY.	UNIT PRICE	TOTAL PRICE

SHPPING METHOD _____

SHIPPING COMPANY _____

TRACKING IN _____

SHIPPING DATE _____

ARRIVAL DATE _____

SUBTOTAL _____

DISCOUNT _____

TAXES _____

SHIPPING _____

TOTAL _____

NOTE :

DATE :
ORDER NO :

ORDER FORM

CUSTOMER NAME _____

ADDRESS _____

EMAIL _____ PHONE _____

ITEM NO	ITEM DESCRIPTION	QTY.	UNIT PRICE	TOTAL PRICE

SHPPING METHOD _____

SHIPPING COMPANY _____

TRACKING IN _____

SHIPPING DATE _____

ARRIVAL DATE _____

SUBTOTAL _____

DISCOUNT _____

TAXES _____

SHIPPING _____

TOTAL _____

NOTE :

DATE :

ORDER NO :

 ORDER FORM

CUSTOMER NAME _____

ADDRESS _____

EMAIL _____ PHONE _____

ITEM NO	ITEM DESCRIPTION	QTY.	UNIT PRICE	TOTAL PRICE

SHPPING METHOD _____

SHIPPING COMPANY _____

TRACKING IN _____

SHIPPING DATE _____

ARRIVAL DATE _____

SUBTOTAL _____

DISCOUNT _____

TAXES _____

SHIPPING _____

TOTAL _____

NOTE :

DATE :

ORDER NO :

ORDER FORM

CUSTOMER NAME _____

ADDRESS _____

EMAIL _____ PHONE _____

ITEM NO	ITEM DESCRIPTION	QTY.	UNIT PRICE	TOTAL PRICE

SHPPING METHOD _____

SHIPPING COMPANY _____

TRACKING IN _____

SHIPPING DATE _____

ARRIVAL DATE _____

SUBTOTAL _____

DISCOUNT _____

TAXES _____

SHIPPING _____

TOTAL _____

NOTE :

DATE :

ORDER NO :

 ORDER FORM

CUSTOMER NAME _____

ADDRESS _____

EMAIL _____ PHONE _____

ITEM NO	ITEM DESCRIPTION	QTY.	UNIT PRICE	TOTAL PRICE

SHPPING METHOD _____

SHIPPING COMPANY _____

TRACKING IN _____

SHIPPING DATE _____

ARRIVAL DATE _____

SUBTOTAL _____

DISCOUNT _____

TAXES _____

SHIPPING _____

TOTAL _____

NOTE :

DATE :

ORDER NO :

 ORDER FORM

CUSTOMER NAME _____

ADDRESS _____

EMAIL _____ PHONE _____

ITEM NO	ITEM DESCRIPTION	QTY.	UNIT PRICE	TOTAL PRICE

SHPPING METHOD _____

SHIPPING COMPANY _____

TRACKING IN _____

SHIPPING DATE _____

ARRIVAL DATE _____

SUBTOTAL _____

DISCOUNT _____

TAXES _____

SHIPPING _____

TOTAL _____

NOTE :

| DATE : |
| ORDER NO : |

ORDER FORM

CUSTOMER NAME _____

ADDRESS _____

EMAIL _____ PHONE _____

ITEM NO	ITEM DESCRIPTION	QTY.	UNIT PRICE	TOTAL PRICE

SHPPING METHOD _____

SHIPPING COMPANY _____

TRACKING IN _____

SHIPPING DATE _____

ARRIVAL DATE _____

SUBTOTAL _____

DISCOUNT _____

TAXES _____

SHIPPING _____

TOTAL _____

NOTE :

DATE :

ORDER NO :

ORDER FORM

CUSTOMER NAME _____

ADDRESS _____

EMAIL _____ PHONE _____

ITEM NO	ITEM DESCRIPTION	QTY.	UNIT PRICE	TOTAL PRICE

SHPPING METHOD _____

SHIPPING COMPANY _____

TRACKING IN _____

SHIPPING DATE _____

ARRIVAL DATE _____

SUBTOTAL _____

DISCOUNT _____

TAXES _____

SHIPPING _____

TOTAL _____

NOTE :

DATE :

ORDER NO :

 ORDER FORM

CUSTOMER NAME _____

ADDRESS _____

EMAIL _____ PHONE _____

ITEM NO	ITEM DESCRIPTION	QTY.	UNIT PRICE	TOTAL PRICE

SHPPING METHOD _____

SHIPPING COMPANY _____

TRACKING IN _____

SHIPPING DATE _____

ARRIVAL DATE _____

SUBTOTAL _____

DISCOUNT _____

TAXES _____

SHIPPING _____

TOTAL _____

NOTE :

DATE :

ORDER NO :

 ORDER FORM

CUSTOMER NAME _____

ADDRESS _____

EMAIL _____ PHONE _____

ITEM NO	ITEM DESCRIPTION	QTY.	UNIT PRICE	TOTAL PRICE

SHPPING METHOD _____

SHIPPING COMPANY _____

TRACKING IN _____

SHIPPING DATE _____

ARRIVAL DATE _____

SUBTOTAL _____

DISCOUNT _____

TAXES _____

SHIPPING _____

TOTAL _____

NOTE :

DATE :

ORDER NO :

 ORDER FORM

CUSTOMER NAME _____

ADDRESS _____

EMAIL _____ PHONE _____

ITEM NO	ITEM DESCRIPTION	QTY.	UNIT PRICE	TOTAL PRICE

SHPPING METHOD _____

SHIPPING COMPANY _____

TRACKING IN _____

SHIPPING DATE _____

ARRIVAL DATE _____

SUBTOTAL _____

DISCOUNT _____

TAXES _____

SHIPPING _____

TOTAL _____

NOTE :

DATE :

ORDER NO :

ORDER FORM

CUSTOMER NAME _____

ADDRESS _____

EMAIL _____ PHONE _____

ITEM NO	ITEM DESCRIPTION	QTY.	UNIT PRICE	TOTAL PRICE

SHPPING METHOD _____

SHIPPING COMPANY _____

TRACKING IN _____

SHIPPING DATE _____

ARRIVAL DATE _____

SUBTOTAL _____

DISCOUNT _____

TAXES _____

SHIPPING _____

TOTAL _____

NOTE :

DATE :

ORDER NO :

 ORDER FORM

CUSTOMER NAME _____

ADDRESS _____

EMAIL _____ PHONE _____

ITEM NO	ITEM DESCRIPTION	QTY.	UNIT PRICE	TOTAL PRICE

SHPPING METHOD _____

SHIPPING COMPANY _____

TRACKING IN _____

SHIPPING DATE _____

ARRIVAL DATE _____

SUBTOTAL _____

DISCOUNT _____

TAXES _____

SHIPPING _____

TOTAL _____

NOTE :

DATE :

ORDER NO :

ORDER FORM

CUSTOMER NAME _____

ADDRESS _____

EMAIL _____ PHONE _____

ITEM NO	ITEM DESCRIPTION	QTY.	UNIT PRICE	TOTAL PRICE

SHPPING METHOD _____

SHIPPING COMPANY _____

TRACKING IN _____

SHIPPING DATE _____

ARRIVAL DATE _____

SUBTOTAL _____

DISCOUNT _____

TAXES _____

SHIPPING _____

TOTAL _____

NOTE :

DATE :
ORDER NO :

ORDER FORM

CUSTOMER NAME _____

ADDRESS _____

EMAIL _____ PHONE _____

ITEM NO	ITEM DESCRIPTION	QTY.	UNIT PRICE	TOTAL PRICE

SHPPING METHOD _____

SHIPPING COMPANY _____

TRACKING IN _____

SHIPPING DATE _____

ARRIVAL DATE _____

SUBTOTAL _____

DISCOUNT _____

TAXES _____

SHIPPING _____

TOTAL _____

NOTE :

| DATE : |
| ORDER NO : |

ORDER FORM

CUSTOMER NAME _____

ADDRESS _____

EMAIL _____ PHONE _____

ITEM NO	ITEM DESCRIPTION	QTY.	UNIT PRICE	TOTAL PRICE

SHPPING METHOD _____

SHIPPING COMPANY _____

TRACKING IN _____

SHIPPING DATE _____

ARRIVAL DATE _____

SUBTOTAL _____

DISCOUNT _____

TAXES _____

SHIPPING _____

TOTAL _____

NOTE :

DATE :

ORDER NO :

 ORDER FORM

CUSTOMER NAME _____

ADDRESS _____

EMAIL _____ PHONE _____

ITEM NO	ITEM DESCRIPTION	QTY.	UNIT PRICE	TOTAL PRICE

SHPPING METHOD _____

SHIPPING COMPANY _____

TRACKING IN _____

SHIPPING DATE _____

ARRIVAL DATE _____

SUBTOTAL _____

DISCOUNT _____

TAXES _____

SHIPPING _____

TOTAL _____

NOTE :

DATE :

ORDER NO :

ORDER FORM

CUSTOMER NAME _____

ADDRESS _____

EMAIL _____ PHONE _____

ITEM NO	ITEM DESCRIPTION	QTY.	UNIT PRICE	TOTAL PRICE

SHPPING METHOD _____

SHIPPING COMPANY _____

TRACKING IN _____

SHIPPING DATE _____

ARRIVAL DATE _____

SUBTOTAL _____

DISCOUNT _____

TAXES _____

SHIPPING _____

TOTAL _____

NOTE :

RETURN TRACKER

Date	Order No	Customer	Return Reason	Tracking No	Received	Refunded

RETURN TRACKER

Date	Order No	Customer	Return Reason	Tracking No	Received	Refunded

RETURN TRACKER

Date	Order No	Customer	Return Reason	Tracking No	Received	Refunded

RETURN TRACKER

Date	Order No	Customer	Return Reason	Tracking No	Received	Refunded

RETURN TRACKER

Date	Order No	Customer	Return Reason	Tracking No	Received	Refunded

MONTHLY SALES TRACKER

Date	Category	Description	Amount	Balance

MONTHLY SALES TRACKER

Date	Category	Description	Amount	Balance

MONTHLY SALES TRACKER

Date	Category	Description	Amount	Balance

MONTHLY SALES TRACKER

Date	Category	Description	Amount	Balance

MONTHLY SALES TRACKER

Date	Category	Description	Amount	Balance

BUDGET

Month Of _____

Income	
Date	Amount

Expenses		
Date	Description	Amount

Total : _____

Total : _____

Profit - _____

BUDGET

Month Of _____

Income	
Date	Amount

Total : _____

Expenses		
Date	Description	Amount

Total : _____

Profit - _____

BUDGET

Month Of _____

Income	
Date	Amount

Expenses		
Date	Description	Amount

Total : _____

Total : _____

Profit - _____

BUDGET

Month Of _____

Income	
Date	Amount

Expenses		
Date	Description	Amount

Total : _____   Total : _____

Profit - _____

BUDGET

Month Of _____

Income	
Date	Amount

Total : _____

Expenses		
Date	Description	Amount

Total : _____

Profit - _____

ANNUAL PROFIT

	Income	Supplies	Marketing	Fees	Profit
JAN					
FEB					
MAR					
APR					
MAY					
JUN					
JUL					
AUG					
SEP					
OCT					
NOV					
DEC					
Total					

NOTES

Date : _____

NOTES

Date : _____

NOTES

Date : _____

NOTES

Date : _____